MOUNT RUSHMORE

Joanne Matte[...]

Rourke
Educational [...]
rourkeeducation[...]media.com

Before Reading:

Building Academic Vocabulary and Background Knowledge

Before reading a book, it is important to tap into what your child or students already know about the topic. This will help them develop their vocabulary, increase their reading comprehension, and make connections across the curriculum.

1. Look at the cover of the book. What will this book be about?
2. What do you already know about the topic?
3. Let's study the Table of Contents. What will you learn about in the book's chapters?
4. What would you like to learn about this topic? Do you think you might learn about it from this book? Why or why not?
5. Use a reading journal to write about your knowledge of this topic. Record what you already know about the topic and what you hope to learn about the topic.
6. Read the book.
7. In your reading journal, record what you learned about the topic and your response to the book.
8. After reading the book complete the activities below.

Content Area Vocabulary
Read the list. What do these words mean?

bust
conservation
controversial
dedication
dynamite
frontier
granite
masterpiece
monument
remote
sculptor
superintendent
tourists

After Reading:

Comprehension and Extension Activity

After reading the book, work on the following questions with your child or students in order to check their level of reading comprehension and content mastery.

1. Why was Theodore Roosevelt controversial as a face for Mount Rushmore? (Summarize)
2. Why did Borglum select Mount Rushmore? (Summarize)
3. What was the process in carving the faces into Mount Rushmore? (Summarize)
4. Why did Robinson want someone who was "more than a stone carver?" (Asking questions)
5. Why is tourism important for states? (Infer)

Extension Activity

You are Gutzon Borglum and have recently been hired to sculpt an amazing attraction in South Dakota. Your employer wants you to sculpt frontiersmen, but you think there are others who may be a better choice. Write a letter to your employer suggesting four other people who would best represent our country and explanations why you chose each person.

TABLE OF CONTENTS

A BIG IDEA

It was 1923 and Doane Robinson had a big idea. Robinson was the state historian of South Dakota. He knew his state was full of natural beauty. It was also an important part of American history during the **frontier** days. However, South Dakota had a problem. It was far away from most major American cities and difficult to get to.

Robinson wanted other people to discover South Dakota, and he thought of a clever way to get them there. Robinson wanted to carve giant statues into the rocks of South Dakota's Black Hills. He believed that these large statues would attract **tourists** to South Dakota. Robinson talked about his idea to everyone he knew. Many people liked Robinson's idea.

Freedom Fact!

At the time, automobiles were becoming popular, making it easier for people to travel. Building giant statues seemed like a great way to attract new drivers to the state.

One of the people Robinson talked to was Peter Norbeck. Norbeck was a U.S. senator, and he had many important connections in the government. Norbeck loved Robinson's idea. Because of his state support, many other people joined the project.

The faces of four great U.S. presidents look out from Mount Rushmore, one of the United States' most powerful symbols.

There was just one big challenge to face. Who would carve Robinson's giant figures? Robinson knew how difficult the job would be. He said, "The fellow who does it must be something more than a stone carver."

Then Robinson heard about a **sculptor** named John Gutzon de la Mothe Borglum. Borglum had a great reputation for creating huge sculptures. In August 1924, Robinson wrote Borglum a letter inviting him to the Black Hills to create a "heroic sculpture of unusual character."

Who Was Gutzon Borglum?

Gutzon Borglum was born in Idaho in 1867 but grew up on the frontier in Nebraska. When he was sixteen, Borglum traveled to San Francisco, California, to study painting. Later, he moved to Paris, where he became a well-known artist. In 1901, he moved to New York and started a new career as a sculptor. Before starting on Mount Rushmore, Borglum sculpted the Saints and Apostles for the Cathedral of St. John the Divine in New York City; a statue of Abraham Lincoln in Newark, New Jersey; a **bust** of Lincoln for the U.S. Capitol in Washington, D.C.; and a statue at Lincoln's burial place in Springfield, Illinois.

1867–1941

When Borglum got Robinson's letter, he was in Stone Mountain, Georgia, carving a **monument** to commemorate Civil War heroes from the Confederate Army. However, Borglum got angry with the people who had hired him for the job. In 1925, Borglum destroyed all his models so no one else could use them and quit the job. Then he headed off to South Dakota.

Gutzon Borglum quit his job carving Confederate heroes into Stone Mountain, Georgia, to take on the job of carving Mount Rushmore.

Doane Robinson had wanted to carve statues of Western frontiersmen into an area called the Needles. The Needles were a group of tall, thin **granite** rocks. However, Borglum didn't think Western heroes were important enough. Instead, Borglum wanted to carve national heroes, such as great American presidents. Borglum also did not want to create his sculpture at the Needles because he believed the stone wasn't strong enough to carve, and large human figures would not fit in the shape of the rocks there.

The Needles in Custer State Park, South Dakota are made of granite.

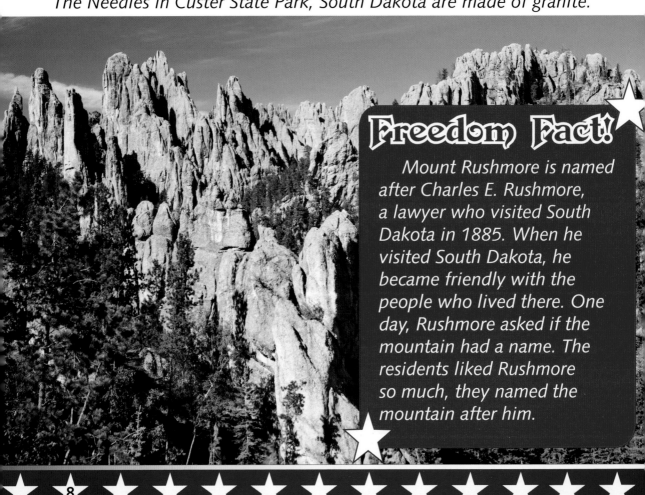

Freedom Fact!

Mount Rushmore is named after Charles E. Rushmore, a lawyer who visited South Dakota in 1885. When he visited South Dakota, he became friendly with the people who lived there. One day, Rushmore asked if the mountain had a name. The residents liked Rushmore so much, they named the mountain after him.

In September 1925, on his second trip to South Dakota, Borglum found the perfect rock face. As he climbed a mountain called Harney Peak, he saw Mount Rushmore. This mountain had everything Borglum wanted. The granite was smooth and a good shape, it was 5,700 feet (1,737 meters) in the air, and it faced the Sun during most of the day. Senator Peter Norbeck was worried that the location was so **remote** it would be hard for anyone to get there, but Borglum insisted Mount Rushmore was the place for his **masterpiece**.

Borglum first saw Mount Rushmore when climbing nearby Harney Peak and knew he had found the spot for his monument.

PLANNING AND PAYING

Before Borglum could start carving, he had to know what figures would be on the mountain. Borglum chose four of America's most important presidents. George Washington was an obvious choice. He was the first president of the United States and was known as "the Father of our country."

Next Borglum chose Thomas Jefferson. In addition to being the third president of the United States, Jefferson had written the Declaration of Independence. President Jefferson also bought a huge area of land from France. This land, called the Louisiana Purchase, doubled the size of the United States.

Abraham Lincoln was also an obvious choice. Lincoln had led the country through its most difficult time, the Civil War. Borglum had already sculpted Lincoln several times and admired him for keeping the United States together during the war.

Borglum's fourth choice was more **controversial**. He picked Theodore Roosevelt, who had been president from 1901 to 1908. Many people did not like Borglum's choice. They thought that Roosevelt had been president too recently. He had died just a few years earlier, in 1919. Borglum said that Roosevelt was important because he developed world trade by opening the Panama Canal and supported **conservation** and business reform.

Theodore Roosevelt
1858–1919

President Theodore Roosevelt sitting on a steam shovel at the Panama Canal.

Choosing his subjects wasn't the only problem Borglum faced. Carving a huge sculpture in a remote mountain would take a lot of money. Borglum promised that his many important and rich friends would donate money to the project, but that didn't happen.

In 1927, Borglum found out that President Calvin Coolidge was spending his summer vacation in the Black Hills. Senator Norbeck and Borglum convinced Coolidge to visit Mount Rushmore for a formal **dedication** to start the project. On August 10, Coolidge spoke in front of about 3,000 people at the dedication. They watched Borglum hang from a swing to drill the first holes in the mountain. The president's support helped raise $54,000 in donations, as well as equipment donations. On October 4, work began on the mountain and continued until December, when it became too cold to continue.

President Calvin Coolidge dedicated Mount Rushmore National Memorial in southwestern South Dakota, on August 10, 1927.

There wasn't enough money to continue work during 1928, so Senator Norbeck continued his efforts to raise money. In 1929, President Coolidge formed the Mount Rushmore National Memorial Commission. The Commission granted matching funds for the project, up to $250,000. Work started up again in June 1929. However, just four months later, in October 1929, the stock market crashed and the Great Depression began. Once again, work stopped.

When the stock market crashed, crowds gathered outside the New York Stock Exchange on what would become known as Black Tuesday.

However, the Great Depression actually helped Mount Rushmore. After President Franklin D. Roosevelt was elected in 1932, he created many government-funded job programs. Many people could be put to work building Mount Rushmore, the roads leading to the site, and other related projects. Therefore, the government supported the project and work went on.

Freedom Fact!

The final cost to build Mount Rushmore was $989,992. The federal government paid most of that money.

Franklin Delano Roosevelt
1882–1945

CARVING IN STONE

Gutzon Borglum had a lot of work to do before he or anyone else could start carving the figures on Mount Rushmore. One of the first buildings constructed at the site was an artist's studio. Here, Borglum created a plaster model of the figures. The model was built on a 1-to-12 scale. Every inch (2.5 centimeters) on the model equaled 12 inches (30.5 centimeters) on the mountain. That meant Borglum's 5 foot (1.5 meter) model could be transferred into a 60 foot (18.2 meter) figure on the mountain.

Borglum also studied the mountain itself. He had to make sure that the rock was strong enough to be carved without falling apart. He found cracks or areas of softer rock in the granite. Borglum had to change his models to work around these problem areas. Borglum changed his models nine times as the work went along.

Someone sculpting a small statue would use a hammer and chisel, but Borglum faced a much bigger job. He had to remove 450,000 tons of rock from a mountain! To do this, Borglum's workers carved with **dynamite**. This process had many different steps.

The first step was for drillers to use jackhammers to make deep holes all across granite that was being carved. Next, powdermen placed sticks of dynamite into the holes and covered them with wet sand. When the men left the mountain for lunch or at the end of the day, the dynamite was lit to blast stone off the mountain. The drillers and powdermen removed 90 percent of the rock from the sculpture this way.

Blasting the mountain

Models in studio

Working on the mountain could be frightening. Workers hung in leather-covered seats that swung them from one spot to another. Callboys watched the workers to see where they needed to move and then told winchmen at the top of the mountain. The winchmen then used rope to lower and raise the seats to the proper position.

Equipment was also sent up and down the mountain. The granite was so hard that the drillers had to change their drill bits after every 3 feet (1 meter) of drilling. A blacksmith at the bottom of the mountain sharpened new bits. He sharpened about 400 drill bits every day.

Freedom Fact!

Workers had to climb up 760 stairs each day to get to their jobs on the mountain.

Once the drillers and powdermen had removed most of the rock, it was time to carve. Platforms, called scaffolds, were attached to the rock. Each scaffold held three or four workers. Workmen called pointers marked the rock to show the workers how deeply to drill. The drillers chipped away the stone to create the faces of the monument.

The final step was called bumping, and it occurred after the stone was shaped. Bumpers used a special air-powered drill to smooth the surface and take away any bumps or rough patches.

Carvers and pointers mark and drill into the rock from the hand-made scaffolding.

Borglum was at the project most of the time. After the powdermen blasted away most of the stone, he studied the faces and made changes in his models for the workers to follow. Sometimes Borglum put on a safety harness and climbed the monument himself to paint marks on areas that needed carving.

Borglum made thousands of changes over the course of the project. Some were small, but others changed the look of the monument completely. At one point, Borglum turned Washington's head by twenty degrees so the Sun would shine on it longer every day.

Freedom Fact!

To make the sculpture's e
look lifelike, workers carved
piece of granite in each pup.
This extra piece of rock catc
the light and helps the eyes
look more natural.

The biggest change was to the Thomas Jefferson sculpture. Jefferson's figure was planned to be on Washington's right. However, after workers removed 90 feet (27.4 meters) of rock, they discovered that the rock was not strong enough to carve. The only way to solve the problem was to move Jefferson to Washington's left side and start over.

Workers began carving Jefferson to Washington's right.

Jefferson

FINISHING TOUCHES

By 1937, Gutzon Borglum was spending more time away from the project. Some of that time was spent meeting with government officials and raising money. Also, Borglum was getting older and his health was not good. In 1938, Borglum's son, Lincoln, became the new **superintendent** at the site. Lincoln had worked on the project from the beginning. He started as an unpaid worker when he was a teenager and, in time, worked on every part of the monument. He was the perfect person to take over his father's job.

Freedom Fact!

Borglum took many safety precautions. Thanks to his carefulness, no one was killed or seriously injured during the project.

In 1939, the funds to finish Mount Rushmore were once again used up, and the federal government had to step in. This time, Congress set a deadline of June, 1940 to finish the memorial. On July 2, Theodore Roosevelt's head became the last figure on the monument to be dedicated. After that, workers spent the rest of 1939 and 1940 polishing the stone. When the job wasn't finished by June, Congress extended the deadline to 1941.

Workers put the finishing touches on Mount Rushmore.

In March 1941, Gutzon Borglum's health failed, and he died in Chicago on March 6. Lincoln Borglum spent the year directing workers and putting the finishing touches on his father's monument. On October 31, 1941, the work was finally complete. Lincoln Borglum made one last trip across the mountain, moving across its face in a swing seat.

Before he died, Gutzon Borglum surveyed workers' progress on Mount Rushmore with his son, Lincoln.

Tourists had started coming to see Mount Rushmore even while it was still being built. When work started, Mount Rushmore was far in the wilderness, with no roads linking it to other parts of the state. That all changed when roads were built to bring workers and equipment to the monument. In 1932, South Dakota received a large amount of money from the federal government to build a highway to Mount Rushmore.

Freedom Fact!

The Mount Rushmore project stopped and started many times. Although it took fourteen years to complete Mount Rushmore, only about six and a half years were spent actually building.

Mount Rushmore is part of the National Park Service. Today more than 2.5 million visitors come to the site every year. Most of them come during the summer months. The Park Service takes care of these visitors and manages a visitors' center filled with information about the monument and how it was built.

In addition, the National Park Service is responsible for caring for the mountain itself. Each year, workers lower themselves onto the mountain to clean the stones, fill any cracks, and make sure every part of the mountain is in good shape. They also use computer imaging to map the monument's features and find any weak spots. Mount Rushmore is a national treasure, and it is a monument that should last for many years to come.

The Avenue of Flags leads to Mount Rushmore. These flags represent all 50 states, the District of Columbia, Puerto Rico, and other U.S. territories.

TIMELINE

1923 —— *Doane Robsinon proposes building a giant monument on the Needles in the Black Hills to encourage tourists to visit South Dakota.*

1924 —— *Sculptor Gutzon Borglum is invited to build the monument. He visits the Black Hills and decides that national figures should be carved into the mountains.*

1925 —— *Borglum selects Mount Rushmore as the site of the project; a dedication ceremony is held and fundraising begins.*

1926 —— *Borglum builds models of Presidents Washington, Jefferson, Lincoln, and Roosevelt.*

1927 —— *A dedication featuring President Calvin Coolidge is held at the site.*

1929 —— *President Coolidge creates the Mount Rushmore National Memorial Commission; Congress passes a law authorizing matching funds for building the monument.*

1930 —— *Washington's face is dedicated.*

1932 —— *South Dakota receives federal money to build a road to Mount Rushmore.*

1936 —— *Jefferson's face is dedicated.*

1937 —— *Lincoln's face is dedicated.*

1938 —— *Lincoln Borglum becomes superintendent of the project.*

1939 —— *Roosevelt's face is dedicated; Congress announces a deadline of June 1940 to finish the monument.*

1940 —— *Congress authorizes a final grant of $86,000 and extends the deadline to 1941.*

1941 —— *Gutzon Borglum dies on March 6.*

1991 —— *Mount Rushmore celebrates its fiftieth anniversary with a final dedication ceremony featuring President George H.W. Bush and nineteen of Borglum's original workers.*

GLOSSARY

bust (BUST): a sculpture of a person's head and shoulders

conservation (kuhn-sur-VAY-shuhn): protecting things like wildlife, forests, or historical objects

controversial (KON-truh-ver-shuhl): causing arguments

dedication (ded-uh-KAY-shuhn): a ceremony held at the opening of a monument or structure

dynamite (DY-nuh-mite): a powerful explosive

frontier (FRUN-teer): the far edge of a country

granite (GRAN-it): a hard, gray rock

masterpiece (MAS-tur-pees): a great work of art, music, or literature

monument (MON-yuh-muhnt): a statue, building, or other structure that reminds people of an event or person

remote (ruh-MOTE): far away

sculptor (SKUHLP-tor): a person who creates figures out of stone or other materials

superintendent (soo-pur-in-TEN-duhnt): someone who is in charge of an organization or project

tourists (TOOR-ists): people who travel to visit places for pleasure

INDEX

SHOW WHAT YOU KNOW

1. Was Doane Robinson's idea to increase tourism in South Dakota successful?
2. Name two reasons Borglum selected Theodore Roosevelt as a figure for the monument.
3. Why did the rock of Mount Rushmore have to be carefully surveyed?
4. How did workers remove most of the rock from Mount Rushmore?
5. How did the Great Depression help the Mount Rushmore project?

WEBSITES TO VISIT

http://www.pbs.org/wgbh/americanexperience/features/biography/rushmore-borglum/

http://www.ohranger.com/mount-rushmore/making-mount-rushmore

http://www.travelsd.com/Attractions/Mount-Rushmore

ABOUT THE AUTHOR

Joanne Mattern has written hundreds of books for children. Her favorite subjects are history, nature, sports, and biographies. She enjoys traveling around the United States and visiting new places. Joanne grew up on the banks of the Hudson River and still lives in the area with her husband, four children, and numerous pets.

Meet The Author!
www.meetREMauthors.com

www.rourkeeducationalmedia.com

PHOTO CREDITS: Title Page © Visions of America; page 5 © iofoto; page 8 © John Mirro; page 8, 14 © Library of Congress; page 8 © New York Times Photo Archive; page 13, 17, 18, 19, 21, 23, 24, 25, © Charles d'Emery courtesy of NPS; page 15 © Elias Goldensky; page 20 © Conrad Fries; page 26 © RiverNorthPhotography; page 27 © James Brey

Edited by: Jill Sherman

Cover design by: Nicola Stratford, nicolastratford.com
Interior design by: Renee Brady

Library of Congress PCN Data

Mount Rushmore / Joanne Mattern
(Symbols of Freedom)
ISBN 978-1-62717-741-2 (hard cover)
ISBN 978-1-62717-863-1 (soft cover)
ISBN 978-1-62717-974-4 (e-Book)
Library of Congress Control Number: 2014935666

Also Available as:

Printed in the United States of America, North Mankato, Minnesota